The Anglo-Saxons

BY

SUSAN HARRISON

EXPLORING BRITISH
HISTORY

©2017
Book Life
King's Lynn
Norfolk PE30 4LS

ISBN: 978-1-78637-164-5

All rights reserved
Printed in Malaysia

A catalogue record for this book
is available from the British Library.

Written by:
Susan Harrison

Edited by:
Charlie Ogden

Designed by:
Ian McMullen

PHOTO CREDITS

The Anglo-Saxons

CONTENTS

WHO WERE THE ANGLO-SAXONS?

When the Romans left Britain around AD 410, tribes came from Germany, Denmark and Holland to take over British land. The tribes were called the Angles, the Saxons and the Jutes. They were powerful warriors. They settled in the south, southwest and north of England and together they became known as the Anglo-Saxons.

Before the Anglo-Saxons arrived, Britain had been part of the Roman Empire. The Anglo-Saxons gradually took control of Britain over the course of around 100 years, splitting the island up into kingdoms with local rulers. The Celts, who had been living in Britain for hundreds of years before the Romans arrived, were pushed back into Wales, Scotland and Cornwall.

THIS MAP SHOWS WHERE THE ANGLES, SAXONS AND JUTES SETTLED IN BRITAIN.

NORTHUMBRIA

MERCIA

EAST ANGLI

ESSEX

WESSEX

KENT

SUSSEX

IT IS BELIEVED THAT PEVENSEY CASTLE IN SUSSEX WAS BUILT BY THE ROMANS AS A FORT TO KEEP THE ANGLO-SAXONS OUT OF BRITAIN. THE ROMANS CALLED IT ANDERITUM.

The first Anglo-Saxon to be King of England was Altheston. He reigned from 927 to 939.

The most important Anglo-Saxon kingdoms in England were Northumbria, Mercia, East Anglia, Wessex and Kent. The kings of these kingdoms often fought each other as they tried to take more of Britain for themselves.

CELTS

ANGLO-SAXONS

ANGLES

SAXONS

JUTES

Nobody wrote much about the story of the Anglo-Saxon invasion at the time it was happening. King Alfred the Great ordered monks to write down the history of the Anglo-Saxons in the 9th *century*, nearly 400 years after the Anglo-Saxons had first invaded. This book is called the Anglo-Saxon Chronicles.

It is believed that a great warrior called Vortigern was the king of the Britons when the Anglo-Saxons first arrived. At first he welcomed the Anglo-Saxons and they helped him to fight the *Picts*, who were a tribe that lived in Scotland. But then two of the Anglo-Saxon leaders, Hengest and Horsa, turned on Vortigern.

AN ARTIST'S IMPRESSION OF HENGEST AND HORSA →

A monk called Gildas wrote down some of the Anglo-Saxon's stories in the 6th century. He wrote that Vortigern fell in love with Hengest's daughter, Rowena, and gave him the county of Kent in return for her hand in marriage.

The Anglo-Saxon rule of Britain lasted for around 600 years. The last Anglo-Saxon king was King Harold II. He reigned from the sixth of January, 1066, to the fourteenth of October, 1066, when he was killed fighting the Normans at the Battle of Hastings.

THIS REPLICA LONGSHIP CAN BE SEEN AT EBBSFLEET IN KENT. IT IS HERE THAT HENGEST AND HORSA ARE BELIEVED TO HAVE FIRST ARRIVED IN BRITAIN.

DYMA GYCHWYN LLWYBR CLAWDD OFFA
OFFA'S DYKE PATH BEGINS HERE

KING OFFA WAS FAMOUS FOR BUILDING A LARGE WALL MADE OUT OF SOIL, KNOWN AS OFFA'S *Dyke*, THAT STRETCHED ACROSS THE BORDER OF MERCIA AND WALES. THE PATH ALONG THE DYKE IS POPULAR WITH WALKERS TODAY. THIS IS THE SIGN AT THE START OF THE WALK.

A t first, the Anglo-Saxons lived in small groups that were mostly made up of people from the same family. Over time, these groups grew larger and began to be ruled by *chiefs* or kings. King Offa, for example, was King of Mercia from 757 to 796. The king was the most powerful person in the kingdom.

After kings, the next most important people were thegns. These were *noblemen* who advised the king and helped him to rule. Most ordinary people were churls. Churls fought for the thegns and farmed their lands. Below the churls were slaves, who were mostly normal people who got captured from other kingdoms during battles.

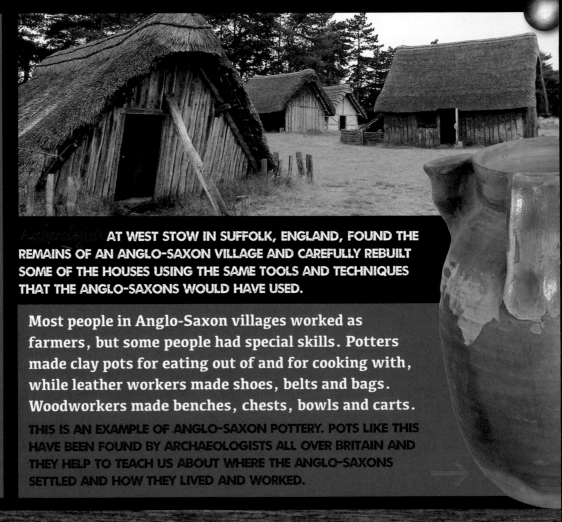

Archaeologists AT WEST STOW IN SUFFOLK, ENGLAND, FOUND THE REMAINS OF AN ANGLO-SAXON VILLAGE AND CAREFULLY REBUILT SOME OF THE HOUSES USING THE SAME TOOLS AND TECHNIQUES THAT THE ANGLO-SAXONS WOULD HAVE USED.

Most people in Anglo-Saxon villages worked as farmers, but some people had special skills. Potters made clay pots for eating out of and for cooking with, while leather workers made shoes, belts and bags. Woodworkers made benches, chests, bowls and carts.

THIS IS AN EXAMPLE OF ANGLO-SAXON POTTERY. POTS LIKE THIS HAVE BEEN FOUND BY ARCHAEOLOGISTS ALL OVER BRITAIN AND THEY HELP TO TEACH US ABOUT WHERE THE ANGLO-SAXONS SETTLED AND HOW THEY LIVED AND WORKED.

Some Anglo-Saxons were also part-time warriors who went into battle when a thegn or a king ordered them to. Training for battle began at an early age. Children would start practising fighting with wooden weapons when they were about eight years old.

THE FAMOUS BAYEUX TAPESTRY, WHICH DEPICTS THE HISTORY OF ENGLAND UP TO THE NORMAN CONQUEST IN 1066, SHOWS ANGLO-SAXON WARRIORS IN BATTLE.

King Offa was also famous for making England's first silver pennies.

Anglo-Saxon warriors followed a strict 'warrior code'. This taught them that a warrior must be brave, strong and loyal to his thegns and king. Every warrior had to be ready to fight to the death for his leader, but he also had to be *humble* and kind.

THIS IS AN EXAMPLE OF WHAT AN ANGLO-SAXON WARRIOR MIGHT HAVE LOOKED LIKE. THEY WOULD HAVE USED THEIR SHIELDS TO MAKE A WALL BY STANDING SIDE BY SIDE AND HOLDING THEIR SHIELDS IN A LINE. →

Most warriors did not have metal armour, but instead wore a thick, leather waistcoat. They attacked with spears, axes and swords, and they protected themselves with wooden shields. Fathers often gave their swords to their sons when they got too old to fight.

THIS SAXON SWORD WAS FOUND IN A GRAVE ON THE ISLE OF WIGHT.

EVERYDAY

ost Anglo-Saxons lived in small villages. Parents, children and grandparents lived together in houses with *thatched* roofs. The houses only had one small room, which had a fireplace in the centre that was used for cooking and heating the house.

ANGLO-SAXONS WOULD GROW CROPS AND ANIMALS SUCH AS SHEEP, COWS AND CHICKENS. THE WOOL FROM THE SHEEP WAS USED TO MAKE CLOTHING.

Thegns would have lived in a large hall in the middle of a village. Sometimes, animals were kept at one end of the hall. Thegns often owned the fields and land around a village.

Anglo-Saxon boys would help on the farms. They would learn how to look after the animals as well as plough the fields. Fathers would often teach their sons how to hunt, fish and fight with weapons. Girls were taught how to cook, brew ale and makes clothes.

Many Anglo-Saxons did not use money and instead used bartering in order to trade. Bartering is a system where a person pays for something they want with something they own, rather than using money. For example, a farmer wanting to buy a cow might offer to swap it for some of his sheep.

 THE MILK FROM FARM ANIMALS, SUCH AS COWS AND GOATS, WAS USED TO MAKE BUTTER AND CHEESE. MAKING THE BUTTER AND CHEESE WOULD HAVE BEEN A JOB FOR THE WOMEN AND GIRLS.

LIFE

Most Anglo-Saxon children did not go to school and most could not read or write. Children were taught the skills they needed to survive by their parents. The children of kings and thegns sometimes had tutors at home.

WEDDING RINGS WERE AN IMPORTANT PART OF ANGLO-SAXON WEDDINGS, JUST LIKE THEY ARE IN MODERN WEDDINGS. THE MAN WOULD ALSO GIVE HIS NEW WIFE THE KEYS TO HIS HOUSE, AS IT WAS NOW HER JOB TO TAKE CARE OF IT.

Anglo-Saxons often got married at a very young age. Girls usually got married when they were around 12 years old and boys when they were around 14 years old. People were allowed to choose who they married, but it was very important that their parents were happy with the marriage.

Anglo-Saxons spoke a language called Old English, which they called Englisc. Many words that we use today come from Old English. For example, the word 'father' comes from the Old English word 'faeder', and 'egg' comes from the Old English word 'aeg'.

THIS TEXT IS WRITTEN IN THE OLD ENGLISH LANGUAGE THAT WAS USED BY THE ANGLO-SAXONS.

For the children of kings and thegns, it was very important that their parents approved of their marriage. This is because kings and thegns wanted to know who was going to carry on their family name.

CRAFTS

Some Anglo-Saxons were *craftsmen*. They would make items that were important in everyday life, such as pots, tools and weapons. They also made things that were *decorative*, such as jewellery.

SOME ANGLO-SAXON CRAFTSMEN MADE COMBS (LIKE THE ONE ABOVE), SPOONS, NEEDLES, PINS AND BUCKLES OUT OF ANIMAL BONES.

A potter would make bowls and plates by mixing together clay, water and sand. *Carpenters* would make handles for farmers' forks and spades, as well as furniture, barrels and buckets.

Carpenters used wood from different types of tree to make different things. For example, the wood from oak trees was often used to make houses. Carpenters would also make spade handles and furniture. They would shape the wood using a device called a lathe.

THIS IS WHAT AN ANGLO-SAXON LATHE WOULD HAVE LOOKED LIKE.

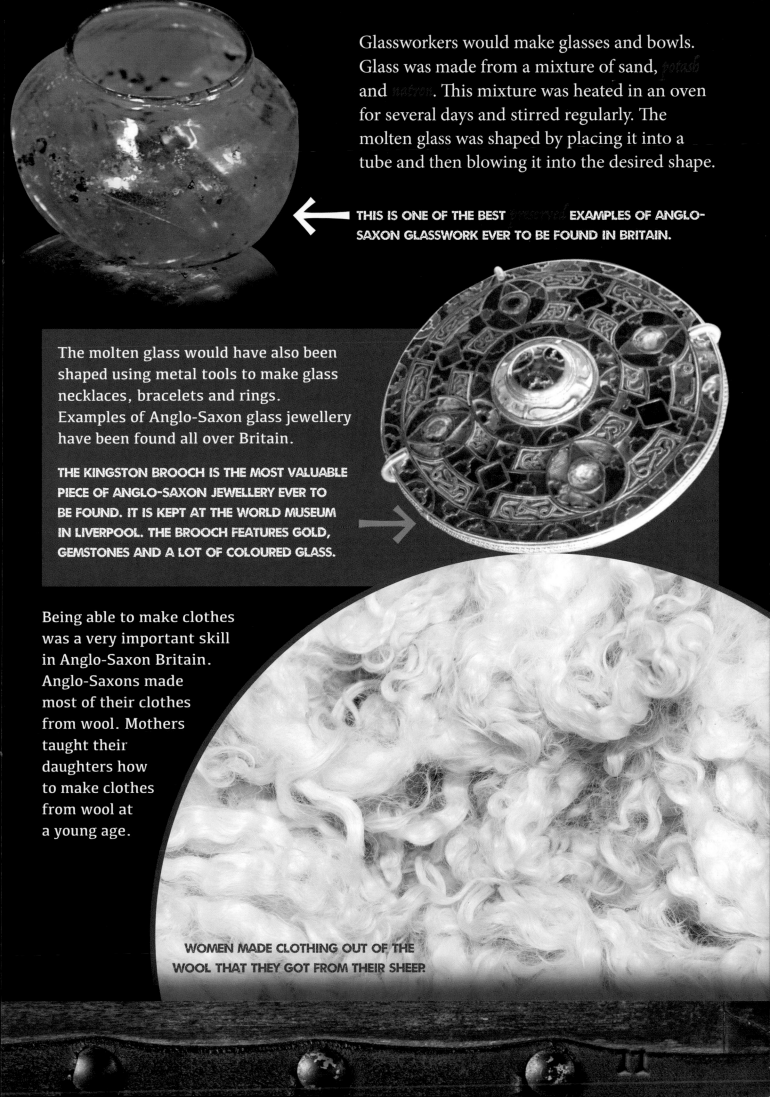

Glassworkers would make glasses and bowls. Glass was made from a mixture of sand, *potash* and *natron*. This mixture was heated in an oven for several days and stirred regularly. The molten glass was shaped by placing it into a tube and then blowing it into the desired shape.

← THIS IS ONE OF THE BEST *preserved* EXAMPLES OF ANGLO-SAXON GLASSWORK EVER TO BE FOUND IN BRITAIN.

The molten glass would have also been shaped using metal tools to make glass necklaces, bracelets and rings. Examples of Anglo-Saxon glass jewellery have been found all over Britain.

THE KINGSTON BROOCH IS THE MOST VALUABLE PIECE OF ANGLO-SAXON JEWELLERY EVER TO BE FOUND. IT IS KEPT AT THE WORLD MUSEUM IN LIVERPOOL. THE BROOCH FEATURES GOLD, GEMSTONES AND A LOT OF COLOURED GLASS. →

Being able to make clothes was a very important skill in Anglo-Saxon Britain. Anglo-Saxons made most of their clothes from wool. Mothers taught their daughters how to make clothes from wool at a young age.

WOMEN MADE CLOTHING OUT OF THE WOOL THAT THEY GOT FROM THEIR SHEEP.

CLOTHES AND JEWELLERY

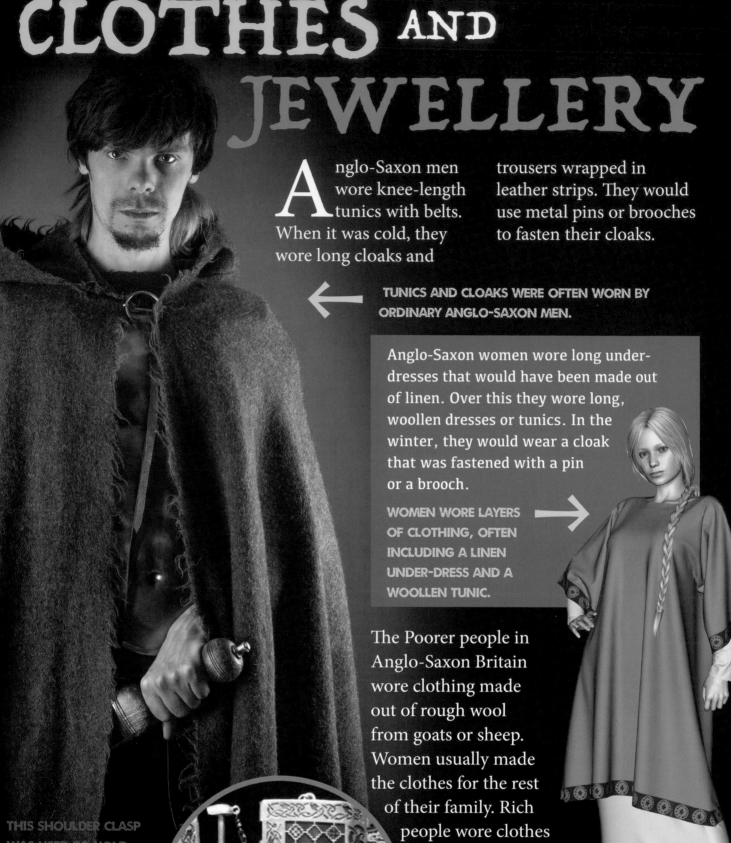

Anglo-Saxon men wore knee-length tunics with belts. When it was cold, they wore long cloaks and trousers wrapped in leather strips. They would use metal pins or brooches to fasten their cloaks.

← TUNICS AND CLOAKS WERE OFTEN WORN BY ORDINARY ANGLO-SAXON MEN.

Anglo-Saxon women wore long under-dresses that would have been made out of linen. Over this they wore long, woollen dresses or tunics. In the winter, they would wear a cloak that was fastened with a pin or a brooch.

WOMEN WORE LAYERS OF CLOTHING, OFTEN INCLUDING A LINEN UNDER-DRESS AND A WOOLLEN TUNIC. →

The Poorer people in Anglo-Saxon Britain wore clothing made out of rough wool from goats or sheep. Women usually made the clothes for the rest of their family. Rich people wore clothes that were made from a finer wool and which were decorated with *embroidery*.

THIS SHOULDER CLASP WAS USED TO HOLD A CLOAK TOGETHER. IT WAS FOUND AT AN *ancient* BURIAL → SITE IN SUTTON HOO, SUFFOLK, ENGLAND.

Rich Anglo-Saxons would have worn jewellery made out of gold and gems. Men would have worn gold belt buckles and brooches to show their wealth. They also had highly decorated sword hilts made just for them.

THE ALFRED JEWEL IS ONE OF THE RAREST AND MOST IMPORTANT EXAMPLES OF ANGLO-SAXON JEWELLERY TO EVER BE DISCOVERED. IT IS INSCRIBED WITH THE WORDS 'AELFRED MEC HEHT GEWYRCAN', WHICH MEANS 'ALFRED ORDERED ME MADE'.

Women wore all kinds of jewellery, such as amulets, necklaces, pendants, rings and bracelets. Sometimes pieces of glass or shell would be included in the design. Rich women wore jewellery that was made from gold and decorated with complicated designs.

THE STAFFORDSHIRE HOARD IS A COLLECTION OF ITEMS FOUND IN STAFFORDSHIRE, ENGLAND. THERE ARE OVER 3,500 DIFFERENT ITEMS, WHICH INCLUDE MILITARY DECORATIONS AND JEWELLERY. THESE ITEMS SHOW JUST HOW SKILLED JEWELLERS, SILVERSMITHS AND GOLDSMITHS WERE IN ANGLO-SAXON TIMES.

The Staffordshire Hoard of gold and silver metalwork was valued to be worth over three million pounds in 2009.

The Anglo-Saxons were very superstitious and many of them wore amulets, or lucky charms, around their necks in order to protect themselves from illness and evil spirits. They also believed that wearing amulets could keep them safe from harm in battle.

THE FULLER BROOCH SHOWS AN ANGLO-SAXON DRAWING OF THE FIVE SENSES; SIGHT, TASTE, TOUCH, SMELL AND HEARING.

FOOD AND DRINK

Anglo-Saxons would have mostly eaten food that they had grown themselves. They would grow wheat, rye and oats in their fields, as well as a lot of different vegetables. Meat would have only been eaten on special occasions and would have come from animals that they reared themselves.

ANGLO-SAXONS WOULD ALSO SOMETIMES HUNT WILD DEER AND BIRDS.

Women would use the milk from cows and sheep to make cheese and butter. Skins from the animals would later be used to make leather goods, such as shoes, belts and bags. These were worn during the winter months to keep warm.

The Anglo-Saxons ate vegetables, such as onions, beans, carrots, leeks and peas, every day. It was an important part of their diet and helped to keep them healthy.

EGGS WERE A REGULAR PART OF THE ANGLO-SAXON DIET. MOST ANGLO-SAXONS WOULD HAVE LOOKED AFTER THEIR OWN CHICKENS.

THEGNS WOULD SOMETIMES HOLD A FEAST FOR THE VILLAGERS AND WOULD OFTEN ROAST A PIG OR A WILD BOAR. THIS WOULD HAVE BEEN COOKED IN THE MIDDLE OF THE THEGN'S HALL OVER A FIRE.

The Anglo-Saxons also ate nuts and fruit. Sometimes the fruit was used to make alcohol for a sweet drink called mead.

The water that the Anglo-Saxons used would have usually come from a river. This water would have been too dirty to drink. Because of this, everyone, even children, would have drunk a weak beer made from wheat or barley. Rich Anglo-Saxons would have also drunk wine brought into Britain from other countries.

ANGLO-SAXONS WOULD HAVE SERVED THEIR DRINKS FROM CLAY JUGS, SIMILAR TO THIS ONE.

Porridge was a staple part of the Anglo-Saxon diet and it was made by mixing oats with water or milk. Bread would have been made using wheat or rye and would have been eaten with cheese and meat or with a stew.

WHEAT AND RYE WOULD HAVE BEEN GROWN IN THE FIELDS AND USED TO MAKE BREAD. BARLEY WAS USED TO MAKE MEAD, WHICH IS A STRONG BEER THAT IS MADE SWEETER BY ADDING HONEY.

Anglo-Saxons used plates and bowls made of wood or clay to eat their meals. They cooked their food in clay pots over a fire. They used knives to cut up food and spoons to eat soup, but they often did not use forks and instead they just used their fingers to pick up their food.

THIS PLATE IS SIMILAR TO THOSE THAT THE ANGLO-SAXONS WOULD HAVE USED. THEY WOULD ALSO HAVE ALSO USED BOWLS AND CUPS MADE OF CLAY.

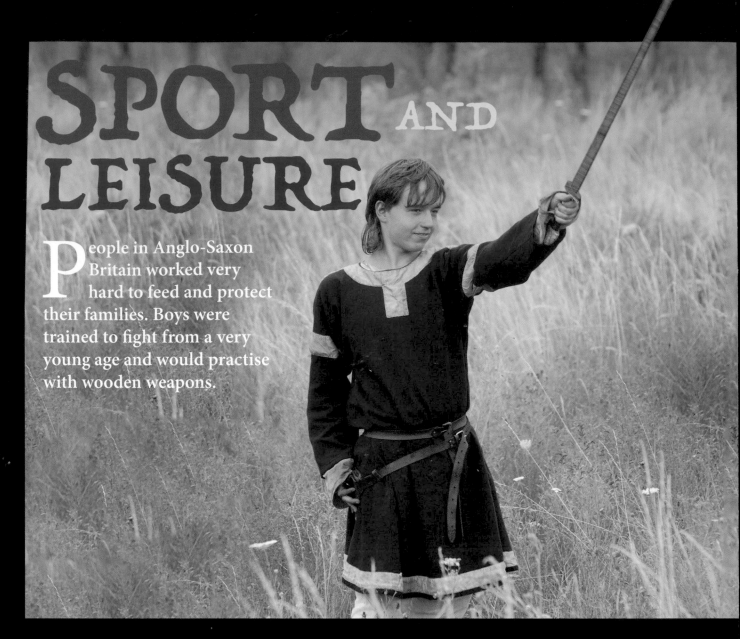

SPORT AND LEISURE

People in Anglo-Saxon Britain worked very hard to feed and protect their families. Boys were trained to fight from a very young age and would practise with wooden weapons.

Anglo-Saxons often got together to take part in sports such as wrestling, weightlifting and ball games. As well as being fun, these sports were important for keeping people strong and they sometimes came in useful during battle.

TUG OF WAR WAS A POPULAR TEAM GAME IN ANGLO-SAXON BRITAIN. IT SHOWED STRENGTH AND IT TAUGHT PEOPLE HOW TO WORK AS A TEAM, WHICH WAS IMPORTANT BOTH IN EVERYDAY LIFE AND IN BATTLE. TUG OF WAR IS STILL A POPULAR GAME TODAY.

As well as playing sports, Anglo-Saxon children also enjoyed board games. The games often used dice and counters. They also played with home-made toys such as wooden animals, rag dolls and spinning tops.

ANGLO-SAXON CHILDREN PLAYED A GAME CALLED KNUCKLEBONES. THIS GAME INVOLVED THROWING PIECES OF BONE INTO THE AIR AND TRYING TO CATCH AS MANY AS POSSIBLE. THE GAME IS VERY SIMILAR TO THE MODERN GAME OF JACKS.

ANGLO-SAXON MEN WOULD GO TO WAR TO FIGHT FOR THEIR KING OR THEGN, SO IT WAS IMPORTANT THAT BOYS GREW UP KNOWING HOW TO FIGHT. AS WELL AS LEARNING HOW TO FIGHT WITH WEAPONS, BOYS EXERCISED BY RUNNING AND CLIMBING TREES AS THIS WAS A GOOD WAY TO KEEP THEMSELVES HEALTHY AND STRONG.

The Anglo-Saxons liked listening to poems about brave warriors. Poems and stories were passed down from one generation to the next by word-of-mouth. Families often sat together and listened to someone tell a great story about a battle that happened long ago.

THIS IS A PICTURE OF AN OLD manuscript OF A POEM CALLED BEOWULF, WHICH WAS WRITTEN IN OLD ENGLISH. IT IS BELIEVED TO HAVE FIRST BEEN WRITTEN DOWN BETWEEN 975 AND 1010, BUT THE STORY WAS BEING TOLD FROM AS EARLY AS 700.

Stories and poems were sometimes sung at meals in time to music. Anglo-Saxons would often play instruments such as , bone flutes and horns.

BEOWULF WAS A GREAT WARRIOR WHO IS SAID TO HAVE KILLED A GREAT MONSTER WITH HIS BARE HANDS. LATER, WHEN HE BECAME KING, HE TRACKED DOWN A DRAGON AND SLAYED THAT TOO.

Game pieces, such as those used for board games, have been found in many Anglo-Saxon graves. They have survived because they were often made from stone or bone, which are both strong materials that take a long time to rot. The boards for the board games were often made of wood, so very few have survived.

The Anglo-Saxons also loved telling riddles, which are questions and guessing games that take some thinking to work out. Riddles would have been something that the whole family could join in with.

An Anglo-Saxon Riddle

I cover the ground like a blanket, and melt in the midday sun.

What am I?

(ANSWER: SNOW)

17

RELIGION AND BELIEFS

When the Anglo-Saxons first came to Britain they were *pagans*. This meant that they worshipped many different gods and goddesses, believing that each of them ruled over a different part of the world.

ODIN IS A VIKING GOD AND WAS CALLED WODEN BY THE ANGLO-SAXONS.

Even though the Anglo-Saxons believed that they would be protected if they worshipped the gods and goddesses, they also wore charms around their necks. These charms were believed to protect against evil spirits, illness and injury.

In 596, the Roman Christian Church sent *missionaries* to Britain to *convert* the Anglo-Saxons to Christianity. These missionaries were led by a monk called Augustine. He began his mission by visiting King Aethelberht of Kent, who had married a Christian princess called Bertha.

By about 700, most people in Britain were Christian and were expected to go to church. Kings who became Christian expected all of their people to become Christian too.

ST MARTIN'S CHURCH IN CANTERBURY WAS ONCE THE PRIVATE CHAPEL OF KING AETHELBERHT'S WIFE, BERTHA. THE KING ALLOWED AUGUSTINE TO TURN IT INTO A CHRISTIAN CHURCH.

THIS IS A STATUE OF KING AETHELBERHT OF KENT, WHO WAS ONE OF THE FIRST KINGS IN ENGLAND TO BECOME CHRISTIAN.

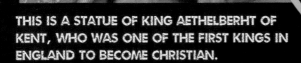

Some of the days of the week in the English language are named after Anglo-Saxon gods. For example, Wednesday is named after the god Woden.

Unlike most people at the time, monks and nuns learned to read and write. Some monks and nuns were also teachers. They help to spread Christianity across the country. It took around 100 years for Christianity to become the main religion in Britain.

The Christian Church in Britain was organised around minsters, which were places where a group of priests, monks and nuns organised worship. Minsters were usually set up by a king or a nobleman who wanted the nuns and monks to pray for him.

A FAMOUS ANGLO-SAXON MONK, CALLED BEDE, WAS THE FIRST PERSON TO WRITE DOWN THE HISTORY OF BRITAIN. MUCH OF WHAT WE KNOW ABOUT THE ANGLO-SAXONS CAME FROM HIS BOOKS.

THE EARLIEST CHRISTIAN MONASTERY WAS AT LINDISFARNE IN NORTHUMBERLAND. THE BUILDING WAS RAIDED IN 793 BY VIKING INVADERS.

SUTTON HOO

In 1938, Mrs Edith Pretty, who lived at Sutton Hoo in Suffolk, asked the archaeologist Basil Brown to dig up some hills that were on her land to find out what was underneath them. Brown dug into the hills and discovered an Anglo-Saxon burial ground.

As Brown started to dig, he discovered that the hills were Anglo-Saxon burial grounds. They contained Anglo-Saxon artefacts and evidence that Anglo-Saxon ships had also been buried there.

THERE ARE THREE LARGE BURIAL MOUNDS AT SUTTON HOO. THIS IS BURIAL MOUND TWO.

THIS BOWL WAS FOUND IN ONE OF THE BURIAL MOUNDS AT SUTTON HOO. →

Under one of the mounds, Brown discovered the perfect form of an Anglo-Saxon ship. The wooden parts of the ship had rotted away, but the shape of the ship was left behind in the sand.

Historians believed that many things in the poem Beowulf were made up, but the evidence at Sutton Hoo suggests that the lifestyle of Anglo-Saxon kings was similar to the description given in the old poem.

IN THE CENTRE OF THE SHIP FOUND AT SUTTON HOO THERE WAS A SMALL WOODEN HUT. INSIDE THE HUT WAS THE LARGEST AMOUNT OF BURIED TREASURE EVER FOUND IN BRITAIN.

It is believed that the ship found at Sutton Hoo may have been the burial ship of Raedwold, the King of East Anglia, who died in the 7th century. There were signs that a large coffin had been buried there and chemicals in the ground showed that there may have been a body.

← THIS HELMET WAS FOUND AT SUTTON HOO AND MAY HAVE BELONGED TO KING RAEDWOLD.

Other items found at Sutton Hoo include jewellery, weapons, armour, cups, spoons and pieces of clothing.

The treasure found at Sutton Hoo has taught us a great deal about how the Anglo-Saxons lived. Everyday items, such as pottery, scraps of clothing, tools and musical instruments, were also found alongside the gold and silver treasures.

THIS GOLD BELT BUCKLE WAS FOUND AT SUTTON HOO, ALONG WITH MANY OTHER VALUABLE ITEMS. →

THIS PURSE LID WAS FOUND AMONG THE TREASURE AT SUTTON HOO. ←

Some people claim to have seen ghosts of Anglo-Saxon warriors near the burial mound at Sutton Hoo.

AFTER THE ANGLO-SAXONS

At the end of the 8th century, the Vikings began to attack England. To begin with, they destroyed the monastery at Lindisfarne, killing many of the monks and taking their treasure. Later, they attacked the east and south coasts of Britain.

ALFRED THE GREAT WAS THE KING OF WESSEX FROM 871 TO 899.

THE VIKINGS CAME FROM SCANDINAVIA, WHICH IS AN AREA OF NORTHERN EUROPE THAT INCLUDES DENMARK, NORWAY AND SWEDEN.

Soon after 871, the Vikings attacked the Kingdom of Wessex. King Alfred fought them back and later made peace with them. He then agreed to divide Britain between them. Alfred took the south and the west of the island, while the Vikings took the north and the east.

In 1016, a Viking called Canute (or Cnut) became the King of England. He died in 1035 and his sons ruled after his death. Finally, in 1042, Edward the Confessor came into power. He was another Anglo-Saxon king. →

THERE IS A LEGEND THAT KING CANUTE THOUGHT THAT HE HAD SPECIAL POWERS AND THAT HE TRIED TO TURN BACK THE TIDE OF THE OCEAN. IN FACT, HE WAS TRYING TO PROVE THAT HE COULDN'T DO THIS! OVER THE YEARS, PEOPLE MUDDLED UP THE TRUE STORY.

When Edward died in 1066, Harold, the Earl of Wessex, became king. Only a few months later, the Normans invaded the country, led by William the Conqueror. King Harold was killed by the Normans during the Battle of Hastings.

The Anglo-Saxon period ended when William the Conqueror became the King of England and the Normans started to settle in England. They started to change Britain with the new culture, ideas and *traditions* that they brought with them.

NORWICH CASTLE WAS BUILT BY WILLIAM THE CONQUEROR BETWEEN 1066 AND 1075. IT WAS BUILT AS PART OF HIS PLAN TO TAKE CONTROL OF EAST ANGLIA. ↓

THIS SECTION OF THE FAMOUS BAYEUX TAPESTRY SHOWS THE MOMENT THAT KING HAROLD WAS KILLED AT THE BATTLE OF HASTINGS IN 1066.

The Vikings now ruled the north and the east of the country. This part of England became known as the Danelaw. Even after Alfred the Great made peace with the Vikings, there was still a lot of fighting between the Vikings and the Anglo-Saxons.

VIKINGS STARTED TO SETTLE IN VILLAGES, SIMILAR TO THIS ONE, ALL OVER THE COUNTRY.

The Normans built over 1,000 motte-and-bailey castles. These castles were built on a hill and were surrounded by a deep ditch, similar to the one in Norwich.

WHAT DID THE ANGLO-SAXONS DO FOR ME?

When the Anglo-Saxons invaded Britain, they brought with them new ideas and skills, many of which lived on long after the Anglo-Saxons were defeated by the Normans.

The Anglo-Saxons preferred to keep away from the Roman towns. They liked to live in smaller settlements and villages. Today, lots of people still live in the small towns and villages that were originally settled by the Anglo-Saxons.

If your name is Alfred, Aidan, Barney, Becky, Harriet, Shelley, Thea or Tracey, then your name comes from an old Anglo-Saxon name.

It is believed that **30%** of white people in Britain are *direct descendants* of Anglo-Saxons.

The Anglo-Saxons were the first group of people in Britain to be fully converted to Christianity. Before this, most people in Britain were pagans. Christian beliefs have been passed down through the generations and most people in Britain today are still Christian.

Many place names in Britain come from Anglo-Saxon place names. For example, if you live somewhere that ends in –bury, -ford, -ham, -ley, -wick or -stun, then it is likely that it was named by the Anglo-Saxons.

Many of the sports that were enjoyed by the Anglo-Saxons are still enjoyed today. For them, sports such as wrestling, tug of war and running were just fun ways of keeping fit for battle. These days, these sports are enjoyed for leisure and competition.

Anglo-Saxon-style jewellery is still very popular today, with people wearing necklaces, rings and brooches that are very similar to those worn in Anglo-Saxon times.

Most Anglo-Saxons were farmers. They understood how to get the best out of their land by planting crops at the right time of the year. Many of their methods were still being used hundreds of years later and many of the same crops, such as wheat, barley and oats, are still grown today.

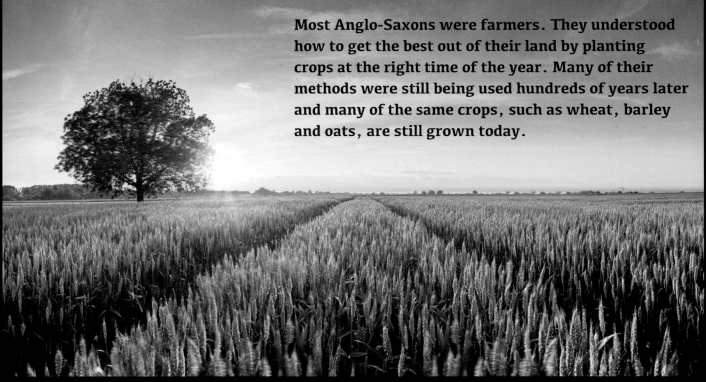

There are many English words used today that originally came from the Anglo-Saxon language of Old English. For example, 'wif' is the Old English word for wife, 'brodor' meant brother and 'hus' meant house.

TIMELINE

The Anglo-Saxons arrive in Britain

449

Aethelberht, the first English king to be Christian, dies

616

The first recorded Viking attack on England occurs in Dorset

789

Athelstan, son of the King of Wessex, defeats a Viking fleet in battle

851

597

Augustine arrives in Kent and begins to convert England to Christianity

627

Edwin of Northumbria becomes the first Christian king in the north of England

793

Vikings attack the monastery at Lindisfarne in Northumbria

Alfred the Great, King of Wessex, dies and is succeeded by his son, Edward the Elder

899

The Viking Canute becomes King of England

1016

King Harold dies at the Battle of Hastings and William the Conqueror becomes the King of England, ending the Anglo-Saxon period and beginning the Norman rule of Britain

1066

886

Alfred the Great agrees to divide Britain and share it with the Vikings

939

Athelstan, the first person to be king over all of England, dies

1042

Edward the Confessor becomes King of England

1066

Edward the Confessor dies and is succeeded by Harold Godwinson

8.   Who were churls?

9.   Who made the first English pennies?

10. Where did most Anglo-Saxons live?

11. What is bartering?

12. What language did the Anglo-Saxons speak?

13. What did boneworkers make?

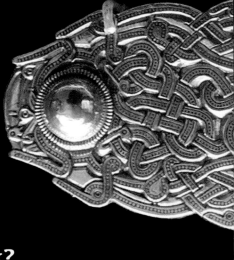

28

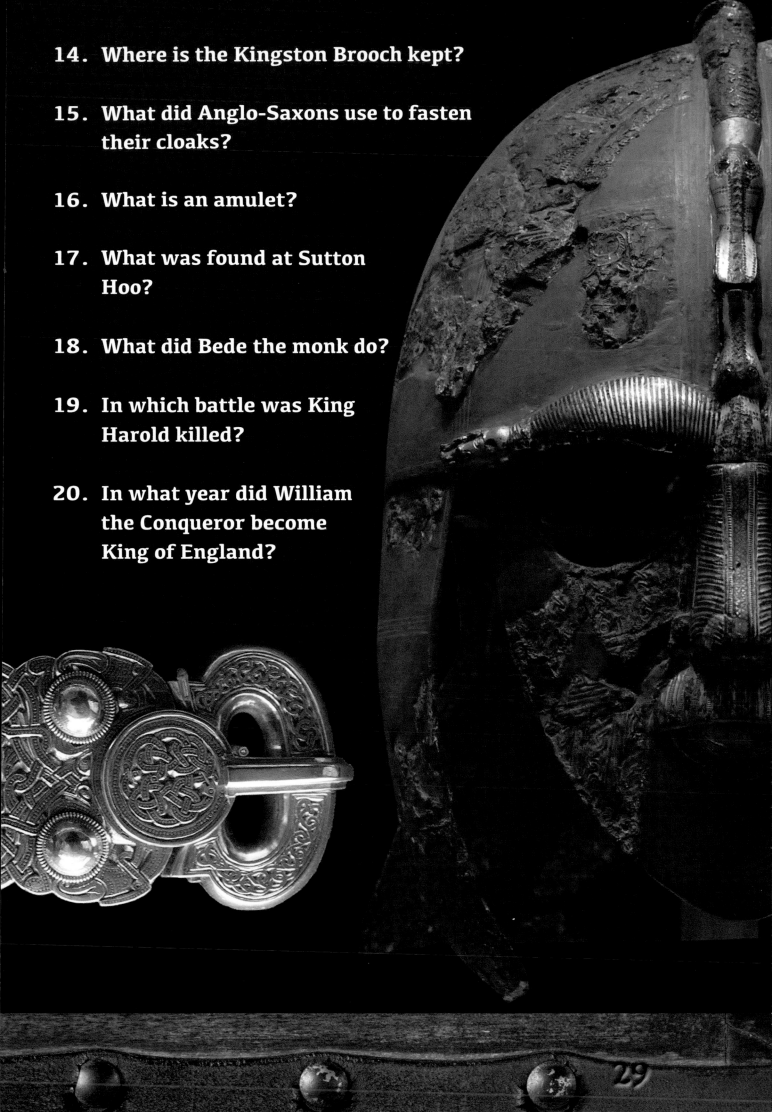

14. Where is the Kingston Brooch kept?

15. What did Anglo-Saxons use to fasten their cloaks?

16. What is an amulet?

17. What was found at Sutton Hoo?

18. What did Bede the monk do?

19. In which battle was King Harold killed?

20. In what year did William the Conqueror become King of England?

direct descendants	genetic relatives of people who lived a very long time ago
dyke	a low wall made of earth that is used for defence
embroidery	a raised pattern sewn into fabric
generation	a group of people from the same family or society who are roughly the same age
hilts	the handles of swords, knives and daggers
humble	having a low estimate of one's importance
kingdoms	countries, states or areas ruled by a king or queen
lyres	stringed instruments that are similar to a harps but much smaller
manuscript	text that has been handwritten by an author
missionaries	people sent to teach people about Christianity
natron	a kind of salt found at the bottom of lakes
noblemen	people who are part of the highest social class
Normans	a group of people from Normandy who became powerful in Europe in the 11th century
pagans	people who believe in and worship a number of different gods
potash	a salty substance, sometimes made from plant ashes soaked in a pot
preserved	maintained in its original state
rear	bring up and care for an animal until it is fully grown
reigned	ruled over a country or kingdom
Roman Empire	an ancient and extensive group of states and cities centred around the city of Rome and the Mediterranean Sea
Romans	people from the Roman Empire
superstitious	believing that a supernatural or spiritual force controls what happens in the world.
thatched	covered with a thick layer of straw
trade	to buy and sell goods
traditions	beliefs or behaviours that have been passed down from one generation to the next
tribes	groups of people linked together by family, society, religion or community

INDEX